AT HOME AND ABROAD WITH

AMARDIP AND REMA

Two Sikh children
visit India

STEVE HARRISON

Macmillan Education

To Warren

The events in this book are a kaleidoscope of the type of experiences enjoyed by children from Britain visiting their parents' place of origin. The events depicted herein are based on true experiences, though some are fictitious, and some of the characters have assumed names.

Acknowledgements

The author and publishers wish to thank and acknowledge the following people for their help in the preparation of this book.

The family of Mr and Mrs Satpal Singh Dulku, David Pritchard, Nirmal Singh, The Sikh communities in Coventry, Amritsar, Naura and Chandigarh, Shirley Parkinson, The Indian High Commission, The headteacher, staff and pupils at Mount Nod Primary School, Coventry, Mrs S. Sangha, Mr and Mrs Puri and Mr and Mrs Gill.

They also wish to acknowledge the following photograph sources:
The Dulku family and David Pritchard pp 8, 9, 13, 16, 17, 20, 21, 24, 25, 36
Fox Photos Limited p 4
Keystone Press Agency Limited p 4
Ann and Bury Peerless pp 32, 33
UNICEF Photos pp 41, 44 — Al Mellett p 44, T. S. Nagarajan p 29
All the remaining photos were taken by Steve Harrison.

First published 1986

Published by
MACMILLAN EDUCATION LTD
Houndmills, Basingstoke, Hampshire RG21 2XS
and London
Companies and representatives throughout the world

Printed in Hong Kong

ISBN 0 333 38610 8

CONTENTS

COVENTRY

Coventry is a large city in the Midlands. It is one of England's major centres for engineering and the famous Jaguar cars produced there are sold world-wide.

During the Second World War Coventry was repeatedly bombed by the German airforce. At the end of the war the whole of the city centre needed rebuilding. The people of Coventry worked hard to make their city attractive and pleasant to live in. New factories, public buildings and the world famous Coventry Cathedral were built. The new

Coventry in ruins. ▶

Coventry as it is today.
▼

factories needed workers, and people from all over Britain moved to Coventry to work.

Coventry's industries continued to expand and still more workers were needed. People from other countries heard about Coventry. They, too, moved to the city to find work. Today Coventry has a very mixed population. Apart from those who moved to the city from various parts of Britain, there are people whose parents and grandparents lived in the following countries: the Ukraine (part of the Soviet Union), Poland, Pakistan, Italy, Kenya, Uganda, India, Hong Kong, Bangladesh and the West Indies.

In this book we shall meet a family who live in Coventry. Satpal Dulku and his wife Surinder moved to the city in 1972. Their son Amardip and daughter Rema were both born in Coventry.

Things to do

People are always on the move. Some move house but stay in the same town, some move from one part of the country to another, and others leave their country and settle in a different one. Men, women and children have migrated from Britain to many parts of the world: North America, South America, Europe, Africa, Asia and Australasia.

Find out where your own family come from. Ask your parents and grandparents about their movements over the last fifty years. Then find out from the other members of your class about their relatives. Mark on a map the places where everyone's grandparents were born.

When and why did your family move to the place where you live now? Compare notes with the rest of your class.

▲
Amardip goes to the local high school.

Rema has learned to ▶
cook Indian dishes.

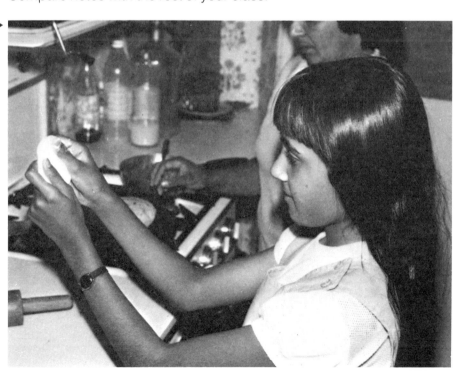

AMARDIP AND REMA

Amardip and Rema both go to school in Coventry. Amardip who is thirteen years old, attends the high school near his home. He is quite good at his lessons, but his favourite activity takes place after school. He is a member of a martial arts club and has won competitions.

Rema is ten and still at primary school. Her school is modern with bright buildings, and large playgrounds and fields. Rema is one of the library monitors. At lunchtime she makes sure that the books are in the correct places on the shelves and that the library is bright and attractive. Jayne, Alison and Peter are also library monitors this term and the four of them work together. Rema enjoys her design technology lessons most of all.

As Rema arrives home before Amardip, she often helps with the shopping. She buys fresh vegetables for the family's meals. Many of the vegetables she buys are strange to most of her classmates. This is because, although Rema and Amardip were both born in Britain, their parents were born in India. Satpal and Surinder still like to eat the kind of food they used to eat in India.

Amardip and Rema are used to eating both Indian and British food. At home they eat Indian food; in school they eat British food.

◀ All the pupils have classes in crafts. Rema does woodwork.

Rema is one of the class librarians.
▼

▲
Rema's favourite
class is design
technology.

Rema shops for
vegetables. ▶

SATPAL AND SURINDER

Satpal Dulku was born in Northern India, in the state of Punjab. His father was a teacher in a village called Naura where Satpal's family had lived for many years. One of his grandfathers was a farmer there and the other was an inspector on the railways. Satpal attended the village school at Naura. He did well at school and went on to college in the nearby town of Jullundur. He studied English, Punjabi and Economics, and later became a teacher himself.

When he was 25, Satpal married Surinder, who was also a teacher. Surinder's brother, Charan, had already emigrated to Britain. When Surinder's father died Charan wanted his widowed mother to join him so that he could look after her. It is the custom in India for the eldest son to look after his parents when they are old. The old lady wanted to

Satpal as a young man in India. In those days he had a beard and wore a turban.

Surinder grew up in the Punjab too. ▶

▲
Surinder married Satpal when they were both in their twenties.

be with her son but did not want to leave her daughter behind. Surinder and Satpal decided that they, too, would go with her to Britain.

Satpal had heard wonderful stories about Britain. He was 27 when he arrived here with his wife and mother-in-law, expecting to find a job as a teacher. Satpal soon discovered that he would not be allowed to teach in Britain without going to college again. He was also told that it would be easier to find a job if he shaved off his beard and cut his hair. He agreed to do so, and soon found a job with the help of Charan at the Ford factory in Leamington. There he earned a good wage and within three years he had saved enough money to buy a house.

While he was working at the factory Satpal studied at night school, and after some years found a job as a welfare officer, helping children in Coventry. Surinder also went back to college, and after finishing her training she got a job as a teacher.

▲
Amardip and Rema were born in Coventry.

Surinder and Satpal when they came to Britain. ▶

THE SIKH RELIGION IN BRITAIN

Even today Satpal sometimes regrets having shaved off his beard and cut his hair short. The Dulku family follow the Sikh religion. Sikh men are not supposed to cut their hair or beards and they are expected to wear turbans.

Amardip and Rema have attended the Sikh temple since they were small. The family go there to worship. The temple is open every day, but most families go on Sundays because this is the day they do not work. The children do not know a great deal about their religion. They can speak a little Punjabi, but cannot read or write it at all.

▲ Sikhs remove their shoes when they enter a gurdwara.

The Guru Granth Sahib is read out loud throughout the day. ▶

Gurdwaras

A Sikh temple is called a **gurdwara** and is open to men and women. All those who enter must have their heads covered and shoes must be removed and placed on a rack. Prayer takes place in a large room. Worshippers sit on the floor facing a highly decorated canopy. Below the canopy sits a Sikh who reads out loud from the holy book of the Sikhs, which is known as the **Guru Granth Sahib**. This book contains the hymns and writings of the Sikh **gurus** (teachers) and other religious teachers, and is written in Punjabi. Worshippers bow before the book and put money into the collection box placed near it.

An important part of the worship is the sharing of **karah prasad**. This is a mixture of flour, sugar and ghee (clarified butter), and all those present are given a little to eat. Every gurdwara has a kitchen attached to it called a **langar**. Sikhs believe that all people are equal and one way of showing this is for everyone to eat together, sharing the same food.

All the worshippers share the karah prasad. ►

Rema bows in front of the holy book.
▼

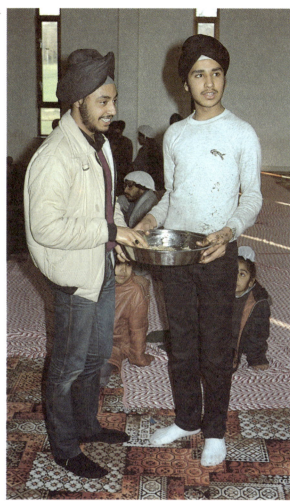

All gurdwaras have a ►
kitchen where food is
prepared for the
worshippers.

A VISIT TO INDIA

Satpal and Surinder worried sometimes that Amardip and Rema did not know more about the Sikh religion, about India and about their many relatives in the Punjab. Satpal and Surinder have always kept in touch with their relatives in India. They wrote regularly and exchanged photographs.

One evening while the family was eating, Satpal asked the children if they would like to visit India. Amardip was excited by the idea. He had always been proud of his Indian origins and of his religion, but he realised that he knew only what his parents had told him. He would learn a lot more if he went to India himself. Rema was not so sure. She was not as interested in India as Amardip. She enjoyed watching Indian films on the television and video, but she thought India would be old-fashioned and dull.

The children could see that their parents wished them to go. Satpal and Surinder began to talk about the people they might visit. As they talked they remembered events from long ago and places they had been to when they were young. Amardip and Rema soon realised that their parents also wanted to visit India, so they agreed to go. It would certainly be a new experience.

Satpal arranged flights for the family. They would spend two weeks together, then Satpal and Surinder would return to Britain to go back to work. The children would remain in India for another three weeks. Amardip and Rema felt happy with this arrangement. Many of their Sikh friends who had visited India had gone alone. They were glad they would have their parents with them for two weeks.

◀ Surinder prepares chapattis.

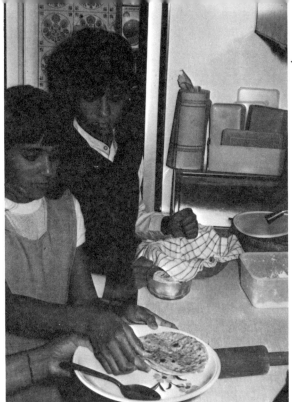

◀ The children cannot wait to start their meal.

Amardip always eats chapattis with his fingers.
▼

Both children had their hair cut before they left so that they would be cooler in the hot sun. It was a cold, wet day when a friend of the family drove them to Heathrow Airport. They flew out on a jumbo jet non-stop to New Delhi, the capital of India. They had packed presents for all their relations, cool clothes to wear and twelve rolls of film for the camera. This was to be a visit to remember.

Rema had her hair cut before she went to India. ▶

दिल्ली DELHI

CHANDIGARH

The Dulku family changed planes at New Delhi Airport. They transferred to an Indian Airlines flight to the city of Chandigarh, capital of the states of Punjab and Haryana. The children had a shock when they left the airport. Chandigarh is a modern city rather like the new towns of Britain. There are wide dual carriageways and large public buildings built of concrete and glass. The shops are in modern shopping precincts and most of them have English names.

Satpal had arranged for the family to stay with one of his cousins, who had a small business in Chandigarh. The house was easy to find because the whole city was planned as a series of areas bounded by straight roads, rather like some American towns. The streets have no names, only numbers. The children noticed that all the houses have flat roofs. Their father explained that in India the roof is like an extra room. People often sleep there on warm nights.

The family enjoyed the few days they spent in the city. It is clean and tidy. They spent their time visiting the leisure lake, the museums and the shops. The children most enjoyed the visit to an exhibition of figures and statues made from rubbish. Amardip thought it sounded awful but he was pleasantly surprised. Broken plates, pots, bottles and many other objects had been used to make all sorts of shapes and figures.

The time came for the family to move on from Chandigarh to Naura, Satpal's village. Satpal warned the children that the rest of India would be very different from Chandigarh.

◀ Chandigarh is a modern city with many public squares.

Most of the shops in Chandigarh have their signs displayed in English.
▼

The models made from rubbish attract thousands of tourists. ▶

There are many fine modern buildings in Chandigarh. ▶

FROM CHANDIGARH TO NAURA

Early in the morning the Dulkus took a taxi to the railway station, where Satpal bought four first-class tickets to Jullundur, the nearest town to Naura. The children felt pleased to be travelling first class. Their mother reminded them that, compared with Britain, train travel in India is very cheap. But though first class in India seems cheap to the British visitor, it is still too expensive for Indians in low-paid jobs.

To get to Jullundur the family travelled first south to Ambala, where they changed trains, then by express, north-west to Jullundur. The whole journey took almost six hours to complete. At Jullundur, Satpal hired a taxi to take them from the station to his home village of Naura. As they drove Satpal kept pointing out places where he had played as a boy. Amardip knew his dad was pleased to be home.

The relatives in Naura were even more pleased. Everyone hugged everyone else. Grandma began to cry, then laugh, then cry again. The children had never met their grandparents before. Now a difficulty arose. It was many years since grandma and grandad had spoken any English. The children could speak only a little Punjabi. Everything they said had to be translated by their parents. Other relatives called throughout the day. Each time Amardip and Rema had to stand up while everyone had a good look at them. Rema's dress was very popular. Most of the Sikh girls were wearing traditional dress and wanted to know why Rema was dressed differently.

Satpal's brother, Kirpal, still lives in the family home. He is married and has three children. Kirpal took Amardip and Rema up onto the roof and read the latest news to them. The children were surprised that the Indian newspapers had reports about what was going on in Britain. Kirpal knew more about Britain than they did about India.

All the relatives were delighted to see the Dulku family.

Kirpal stretched out on a charpoi and told the children what had been in the news since they left Britain.

Things to do

Collect a selection of daily newspapers and check through them with a group of friends. How many stories are about Britain and how many are about other countries?

Do some newspapers have more news about the rest of the world than others? What kind of news about other countries do they include?

Write down some of the things about Britain that you would like foreigners to read in their newspapers. How do they compare with the articles you have read in your papers when they report on other countries, for example America, India, France or Nigeria?

Amardip and Rema's two youngest cousins stayed indoors, out of the hot sun.

AMARDIP AND REMA VISIT A VILLAGE FAMILY

Uncle Kirpal woke the children early the next day. They had asked him to take them around the village. Kirpal explained that the Dulkus are rich farmers. They live in a nice house, but not everyone in the village is so lucky.

He led the children along one of the narrow streets in the poor part of the village. They visited a man whose house was nothing like Kirpal's. It was made of brick but there was no mortar holding the bricks together. He seemed very poor. The man explained to the children that he used to be a farmer in the village. Unfortunately he owned a very small plot of land and could not grow enough food for his family. He had sold his land to one of the richer farmers and found a job in the city driving a tonga. A tonga is a two-wheeled vehicle drawn by a horse which can carry two or three passengers.

The children were asked if they would stay for something to eat and drink. Rema said to Kirpal in English that it seemed unfair for this poor man to be giving them a meal. Kirpal replied that the man would be

Kirpal and the children visited a family who lived in the poor part of the village.

▼

The old lady
prepared
rice for the visitors.

upset if the children refused. Visitors are always offered food and
drink in India. The children thanked the man and an old lady prepared
some rice. She cooked it over an outdoor oven made of clay which was
heated by burning straw. A younger woman boiled water for tea over
a smaller oven, using dried cow dung as fuel.

Kirpal explained to the children that shortage of fuel is a problem in
Indian villages. Because of this, cow dung is collected, rolled into balls
and baked hard into cakes by the sun. It is a good fuel, but if people
burn it there is less dung to be used as fertiliser on the land.

Water for tea was
boiled over an oven
using cow dung as
fuel.

As soon as the children left, the family went back
to work.

19

THE VILLAGE SCHOOL

One morning Satpal decided he would take Amardip and Rema to see his old primary school. The children followed their father through the village but burst into laughter when they arrived at the school. The reason they laughed was that there was no school there, just an empty building.

AMARDIP   Well Dad, your memory is not as good as you thought.

REMA   At least in this school you'd never get any of your work wrong. You could sit here all day and never make a mistake!

SATPAL   That's enough, you two. Obviously the school has moved.

Satpal was right. The school had been moved to a new building. Like many people who leave their home village, Satpal had forgotten that things change. He had expected Naura to be just as it was when he left, but there had been progress in the sixteen years since he moved to Britain.

▲
At lunchtime the children queue for their school dinner. Can you identify the Sikh boys in the picture?

20

▲ One little girl had learned to write the name of the village in English.

▲ The children went to the village post office to post some letters to their friends in Britain.

When they reached the new school the pupils were out playing. Half the pupils at the school are Sikhs, half are Hindus. It is easy to tell the Sikh boys from the Hindu boys. Sikhs do not cut their hair; they tie it up on top of their heads. Many of the pupils were buying their school dinner. Food is laid out on a table at lunch time and soup, vegetables and fruit are available. The children pay for what they want each day.

Later Satpal and the children went into a classroom to watch the lessons taking place. Children in primary school do not learn English, but one little girl surprised Amardip and Rema by writing the name of the village in English on her board. In school the children write on wooden boards. To prepare the boards they first dampen them, then rub clay onto them and leave them to dry. When they are dry, they can write on the boards using black ink. When the teacher has checked their work the children wash off the writing and begin another piece of work. 'Until I came here I thought all school children used pen and paper', remarked Rema. 'It's funny how we always expect everyone else to do things the same way as us.'

VILLAGE LIFE

Amardip was looking out across the village from the roof of Kirpal's house. He asked his uncle why the houses in the village were built so close together.

KIRPAL There's not much space for houses, Amardip. Land is needed for growing food. We build upward in the village, adding an extra floor if we need more space. Look over there and you can see how some houses are higher than others. The roof is often used for storage. Many people keep animal feed and fuel there.

AMARDIP (*pointing*) Uncle, why is that narrow street over there made of brick?

KIRPAL Well, under the bricks there's a sewer where all the water can drain away when the rains come. Of course, at this time of year it doesn't matter much.

AMARDIP I see. And what about work? What sort of jobs do the villagers do?

KIRPAL A lot of people go to work in the city. The ones who do work in the village are either farmers or farm labourers. At this time of year, though, there's little work to be done on the farms, so many of the labourers do craftwork to earn a bit of money. Come, I'll show you.

◀ Some of the streets are paved with bricks. The flat roofs are used for storage.

This labourer weaves cloth on a simple loom to make a little money when there is no work on the farms.
▼

22

The cotton must be spun before cloth can be woven. ▶

They went down from the roof and Kirpal took Amardip to a house where a labourer was weaving cloth on a very simple loom. Outside, an older man was spinning cotton. Both men were farm labourers who could find no work on the land.

On the way home Amardip and his uncle passed the village well where some of the poor women were doing their washing. These days, however, most Punjabi villages have piped water or pumps.

◀ A woman does her washing at the village well.

In the middle of the day even the buffalo need to sit in the shade.
▼

THE LAST DAYS IN NAURA

After school the village children play games. Amardip and Rema recognised some of the games. Cricket is very popular in the village. Hockey is also played by some of the older children. There were other games that Amardip and Rema had never seen before. They stopped to watch a group of boys playing a ball game. One boy threw the ball at a pile of stones inside a circle drawn in the sand. The ball hit the stones, which toppled over, and the ball bounced away. The thrower had to rebuild the pile of stones before the others reached the ball and threw it back.

Satpal told everyone how good he used to be at this game when he was a boy. Rema asked her father to show them. Satpal agreed. It was many years since he had played and everyone smiled as he prepared to throw. One shot was all he needed: the pile dropped perfectly and the ball shot off at high speed giving him plenty of time to rebuild the pile of stones. After all these years he had not lost his touch.

The visit to Naura was coming to an end. There were other places to visit, other people to see. The two children and their parents made a final tour of the village. Surinder had to collect a pair of sandals from

◀ Some of the village boys were playing a ball game Amardip and Rema had never seen before.

The old shoemaker makes shoes to fit exactly.
▼

24

an old shoemaker which she had ordered on her first day there. The shoemaker had promised to have them ready before the family left. The shoes were a perfect fit.

Grandad had phoned for a taxi from the city. The family finished packing their bags and waited at the front of the house. The visit had been a great success, but the time had passed too quickly. The grandparents and relatives wished they could have seen more of the family from Britain. There were tears and hugs when the taxi arrived. The children looked back as they left the village. Their relatives did not stop waving until the taxi was completely out of sight. The family would like to have stayed longer, but they had to leave. They were on their way to a wedding, and that was something not to be missed.

Things to do

People of different countries enjoy playing different games. Why do you think cricket became popular in India?

A game that is now very popular in Britain was invented in India by British soldiers. Find the name of the game. *Clue* The game is played indoors on a green surface; the black is more valuable then the red.

Why is cricket more popular than football in India?

A taxi arrive to take the Dulkus to Jullundur. Satpal found it very hard to say goodbye to his family.

▼

A SIKH WEDDING

A cousin of Surinder was to be married to a young man from Jullundur. When the bride's family heard that the Dulkus would be in India they invited them to the wedding. The marriage had been arranged by the families of the bride and groom. The couple had met and were quite happy with the arrangements.

Satpal and Amardip went to the groom's house in the morning. The groom had got up early, said his morning prayers and was preparing for the wedding. He put on a new suit, just like those worn in Britain. His red turban was covered with gold decoration and he had a garland round his neck. The garland was made up of Indian rupee notes, given to him by friends.

A magnificently decorated white horse was brought to his house. The groom mounted the horse and rode towards the bride's home where the wedding was to take place. Amardip and many other guests followed on foot. As they neared the bride's house they heard the sound of an Indian band. The groom entered the house carrying a scarf. He went into the room where the ceremony was to take place and sat at the front, near to the holy book.

The bridegroom rode ▶
to the bride's home
on a white horse.

The bride's face was hidden by her purple dupatta.

Surinder and Rema had been with the bride while she dressed in her new clothes. Everyone turned to look at her as she entered the room. Her face was covered by a purple dupatta embroidered in gold. With her was one of her sisters who acted as her bridesmaid. The two women sat down at the front of the room.

While the wedding ceremony took place there was a great deal of activity outside. Food was being prepared for the many guests. A Sikh wedding is not just for two people, it involves both their families and all their relatives.

All the family had been busy preparing food for the hundreds of guests.

THE WEDDING CEREMONY

The bride and groom sat close to the holy book, the Guru Granth Sahib. The bride's father placed a garland of fresh flowers on the Granth. He also put garlands around the necks of his daughter and the bridegroom. The bride then took hold of one end of the scarf which the groom had brought.

An elderly Sikh man read four passages from the Granth. After each reading the bride and groom bowed to the holy book. A hymn was sung and then the groom led his bride around the Granth four times. The ceremony ended with the sharing out and eating of karah prasad.

After the wedding all the guests offered their congratulations and the celebrations began. There were speeches, feasting and singing, and the band played until late at night. Like marriages everywhere, it was a joyful occasion for everyone present. Amardip and Rema thoroughly enjoyed the whole evening.

A band played in the ▶ centre of the village all day and long into the night.

Things to do
Have you ever been to a wedding in Britain? In what ways was it similar to the one Amardip and Rema went to, and in what ways did it differ? Make a list. To help you start, think about these questions:

Did anyone wear special clothes? Who? What kind of clothes?
Who else was at the wedding? Friends? Relatives?
Was there a special book used during the ceremony?
What happened after the wedding ceremony?

HEALTH AND NUTRITION

▲
This child is having an early morning wash at a pre-school centre.

Rema was surprised that she had not seen any starving people. Many of her school books on India showed pictures of starving people. Television had also given her the idea that many people in India do not have enough to eat. She asked her mother why they had not seen any people suffering from starvation.

'India is an enormous country with deserts, mountains, jungles, rich fertile fields – everything!' explained Surinder. 'There are parts of India where the land is very poor and rain hardly ever falls. It's almost impossible for people there to grow enough food for their families. Here in the Punjab we are in the most fertile region of India; the soil is good, the rain falls at the right time and the farmers produce more than enough food.

'Even so it is very important that people look after their health. Most people in India live in villages. Few villages have doctors living in them, so doctors, nurses and midwives visit the villages regularly. Mothers are taught how to look after their children's health. When I was expecting you I went to the antenatal clinic in Coventry. Later the nurse visited us at home to make sure we were both healthy. In the villages here, the travelling nurse does the same thing.'

▲
Most villages have a local midwife who visits pregnant women to make sure they are fit and healthy.

▲
The visits continue after the baby is born; both mother and child need care and attention.

AMRITSAR

Satpal and Surinder had only two more days in India. Before they left for Britain they wanted to take their children to the holy city of Amritsar. The family caught a train from Jullundur, then took a taxi from the railway station into the city along a modern dual carriageway. It still seemed strange to the children to see cars, buses and bullock carts all sharing the same roads. Even in the centre of great cities in India you will find farmers driving along in bullock carts.

The building of the city

Guru Ram Das, the fourth guru of the Sikhs, wished to build a city. He bought some land and dug a lake there with the help of his followers. Then they built small huts where they lived, worked and worshipped together. Many Sikhs came to live there and later the city was named Amritsar, which means 'pool of nectar'. Guru Arjan, the son of Ram Das, built a gurdwara at Amritsar which is known as the Golden Temple. This is the most important gurdwara and is a place of pilgrimage for Sikhs all over the world.

Today Amritsar is a centre of trade and learning, and has many famous buildings besides the Golden Temple, including a tower, a castle, a museum and a university.

Even in the centre of modern cities you can see farmers driving their bullock carts.

The taxi driver took the family to the Golden Temple. Surinder hurried over to a flower seller and bought a garland of marigolds to take into the temple. They walked through the main entrance gate and removed their shoes. They had already covered their heads. The steps on the far side of the gate are made of marble but Amardip and Rema still found

▲

Most visitors to the Golden Temple buy marigolds to take in with them.

A woman stops to pray by the entrance. ▶

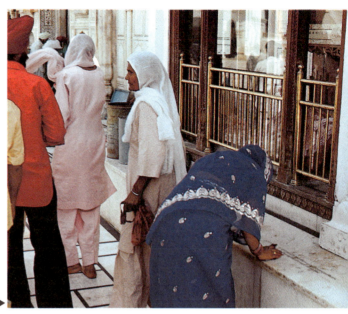

them very hot: the midday sun was shining straight down. As people entered the holy area they performed their own acts of worship. Many people bowed and kissed the marble steps. Others put their hands together to pray.

The temple stands in the middle of a lake around which is a marble pavement. Many Sikhs were bathing in the lake. Cleaning the body before worship is very important. Satpal did not want the family to enter the Golden Temple straight away. He wanted his children to learn about the history of the Sikh religion and of the temple. He led them to a beautiful white building on the far side of the lake. As they entered Satpal said, 'In here you will learn about our religion. This is the museum of the Sikhs.'

Many visitors to the Golden Temple bathe in the lake. ▶

31

SIKH HISTORY

The museum at Amritsar is full of paintings, photographs and objects which help visitors to learn about the religion and history of the Sikhs.

The Sikh gurus

The Sikh religion began with the teachings of a man called Nanak who was born in 1469. The word Sikh means 'disciple', and Sikhs are followers of their gurus, or religious teachers. Nanak taught that all people, regardless of class, religion or sex, could experience God. He did not set out to start a new religion, but from his teachings Sikhism developed.

Before he died Guru Nanak chose a successor. In all there were ten Sikh gurus, each of whom passed the teachings of the first to their Sikhs. The succession ended with the death of Guru Gobind Singh in 1708. When he died he told the Sikhs that they needed no guru other than the holy book, the Granth. Since his death Sikhs have called the book the Guru Granth Sahib.

Below left: Guru Nanak, the first Sikh guru.

Below right: Guru Gobind Singh, the tenth Sikh guru.

At first the Sikhs were friendly with Muslims and Hindus. The Mughal Emperor Akbar, who ruled India, was a Muslim, but he wanted people of all religions to live together in peace. The hymns of the gurus were written down, gurdwaras were built and in 1589 the building of the Golden Temple was completed.

In 1606 Guru Arjan, the fifth guru, became the first Sikh martyr. He was tortured and killed by Akbar's son, the Emperor Jahangir, who did not like the guru and his religion, and resented his influence

among the people he ruled. Guru Tegh Bahadur, the ninth guru, was put to death by another Mughal emperor, Aurangzeb. Aurangzeb, the great-grandson of Akbar, was not tolerant of other religions and persecuted those who would not convert to the Muslim faith. About 500 Hindus came to Guru Tegh Bahadur for help. The guru tried to convince the emperor to allow the Hindus to practise their faith, but the emperor only offered him a choice between conversion to the Muslim faith or death. The guru chose to die and was beheaded in Delhi in 1675. Many of his followers were killed in terrible ways. Amardip and Rema looked at the pictures on the wall. They could not believe that such awful torture and killing had happened. 'Why didn't the Sikhs fight back?' asked Rema.

The Sikhs did begin to fight. Guru Nanak had taught that people should live in peace, but Tegh Bahadur's son, Guru Gobind Singh, decided it was time to fight. He said the Sikhs must become a brotherhood, ready to fight for one another. Every man must take the name Singh, which means 'lion', and every woman the name Kaur, which means 'princess'. He ordered his followers not to cut their hair, to wear a steel bracelet, to carry a sword and to wear shorts so that they could fight more easily. Their long hair was held in place by a special comb and turbans were worn. The turban showed that a Sikh was not afraid to be recognised.

Amardip and Rema had learned a great deal about the Sikh religion during their visit to the museum. Their parents felt it was important that the children should know about the past. Now it was time to enter the Golden Temple itself. The museum contains other pictures and objects which bring Sikh history up to date. The triumphs of Ranjit Singh are shown. Photographs of the massacre of Sikh men, women and children by British soldiers under General Dyer are also displayed.

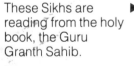
These Sikhs are reading from the holy book, the Guru Granth Sahib.

THE GOLDEN TEMPLE

The family left the museum and walked along the marble pavement. The temple stands in the centre of the lake and can only be reached by crossing a causeway. The Dulkus joined the Sikhs who moved in single file across it.

The Harmandir

After the lake had been dug at Amritsar, Guru Arjan decided to build a gurdwara where everyone could worship. The gurdwara was called the **Harmandir**, which means 'temple of God'. It has four entrances, one on each side, to show that it is open to all people, Sikh or non-Sikh.

The outside walls of the gurdwara are covered with gold leaf, which is why people call it the Golden Temple. The inside of the gurdwara is also beautiful, with fine paintings and marble inlaid with precious stones. The holy book, the Guru Granth Sahib, is in the centre of the gurdwara on the ground floor. It is covered with a canopy which is decorated with jewels. The book is read aloud from morning to night.

At the end of the sixty-metre causeway the Dulkus entered the Golden Temple. Surinder placed her marigolds near the Guru Granth while Satpal and the children put some money on the ground in front of the book. Then the family began to climb up the marble steps to the next floor. They rested on the upper floor for a while and looked down from a balcony to where the book was being read.

The Golden Temple stands in the centre of a great lake.
▼

To reach the temple, ▶
Sikh pilgrims pass
through the gateway
onto the causeway.

After a time the four of them returned across the causeway. Their visit to the Golden Temple was not yet at an end. Every gurdwara has a kitchen attached. Sikhs believe that free food and lodging should be provided for all visitors and travellers, Sikh or non-Sikh. Many of the buildings around the lake contain rest-rooms and beds for the night. Satpal showed the children the old kitchens where thousands of chapattis are prepared every day. Some people prepare the flour, some keep the fires burning, while others cook the chapattis. Brand new kitchens have also been opened in the temple, but there are so many visitors that both kitchens are used.

The Dulkus gave more money to the temple as they left. Satpal and Surinder have good jobs and can afford to help the temple provide for the poor people who visit.

◀ All day long chapattis are prepared for the large
number of visitors. These chapattis are being
cooked in the old kitchens.
▼

AMARDIP AND REMA SAY GOODBYE TO THEIR PARENTS

It was almost time for Satpal and Surinder to go back to England. The day before they left the family visited the fort and the new university in Amritsar. In the evening they went to their hotel for a meal. It would be the last meal the family would have together in India.

Since their arrival in India the children had eaten only Indian food. When the waiter came to the table they were surprised when he asked them if they would like the Indian or the English menu. The children chose the English menu, their parents the Indian. Amardip ordered bacon, egg and chips; Rema chose fish fingers, chips and beans.

The waiter explained that Sikhs from all over the world come to Amritsar. There are Sikhs from Singapore, South Africa, Canada, America and Britain. Many of these people have never lived in India and are used to eating different kinds of food, so most hotels provide an international menu. Alcoholic drinks are also available, although Sikhs are not supposed to smoke or to drink alcohol. Many Sikhs do drink, however, and Satpal enjoys a glass of beer when he is in Britain.

Early next morning the family had a last look at the Golden Temple and Surinder took a photograph of her husband and children standing by the lake. At lunchtime Satpal's cousin, Balwant Singh, arrived in Amritsar. The children would spend the next three weeks with him. He drove the family to Amritsar Airport. The children said goodbye to

Surinder took a photograph of her family in front of the Golden Temple.

▼

their parents and wished them a safe journey. Surinder warned the children to be on their best behaviour.

As their mother and father moved towards the plane the children looked near to tears. Balwant soon changed that. 'Come on, you two,' he ordered. 'You can have Thumbs-up, Campa-Cola or Double 7. Last one to the refreshment bar pays!' After a drink they walked back to Balwant's car for the journey to his village. The next few days would be restful compared with the last two weeks – time to relax and practise a little Punjabi.

The children ate English food but their parents chose Indian dishes.

▼

Things to do

	Jan	Feb	Mar	Apr	May	June	July	Aug	Sept	Oct	Nov	Dec
Maximum (°C)	19	23	28	34	39	40	36	34	34	32	27	21
Minimum (°C)	5	7	12	16	21	25	26	25	23	17	9	5

The chart above shows the maximum and minimum temperatures in Amritsar throughout the year. Using the information given in the chart, draw a temperature graph for Amritsar. Then find out the monthly temperatures where you live and draw a similar graph for your own area. Compare the two graphs.

In which months do you think the refreshment bars in Amritsar sell the most Campa-Cola?

Are there any months when the nights (minimum temperatures) in Amritsar are warmer than the days (maximum temperatures) in your area?

The night temperatures from May to September do not drop below 20°C. Where would you choose to sleep in that heat? Would you need blankets?

Now look at these rainfall figures for Amritsar.

	Jan	Feb	Mar	Apr	May	June	July	Aug	Sept	Oct	Nov	Dec
Average rainfall (mm)	38	11	26	9	11	32	169	168	106	54	10	15

Does this information make you change your mind about where to sleep?

BALWANT'S VILLAGE

Balwant's village is about ten kilometres from Amritsar. His family are landowners and they live in a comfortable house. Amardip was surprised at the size of the house. He had expected his relatives to live in small houses, but he had been wrong. A part-time cleaner and a woman who washes the dishes come in every day to keep the house clean. They are poor women who live on the far side of the village.

Whole families work together building roads. Many of these people come from other parts of India to find work in the Punjab. ▶

Bricks are dried in the sun before being fired in ovens.
▼

Balwant explained to the children that India has a very large population. In some areas there are no jobs so people have to move to find work. The Punjab is a rich area and people from all over India move to the Punjab and do the lowest paid jobs. Balwant took Amardip and Rema to see the new road that was being built near the village. In Britain much of the work would be done by machines but in the Punjab, road-building provides work for people from South India, who migrate to the area to find work.

Close to the road was a brickworks. Families work as a team to produce the bricks. Clay, straw and water are mixed together and pressed by hand into moulds to form bricks. The bricks are then stacked to dry in the sun. After baking in the sun the bricks are fired in large ovens and then sold. Many people in India – men, women and children – work very long hours to earn enough money to live on.

Rema noticed many one- and two-person enterprises. Two men were selling nuts by the roadside. A man was repairing bicycles on the pavement and a metalworker was making kitchen tools. Years ago he would have made different kinds of tools for the local people. These days he makes hundreds of identical tools which he sends to the city, where they are sold in shops. Villagers travel to the city by bus to buy what they need.

Before they returned to his house, Balwant took the children to visit the village gurdwara. The gurdwara was beautiful inside and the Granth was kept beneath a beautiful canopy. It reminded the children of their gurdwara in Coventry.

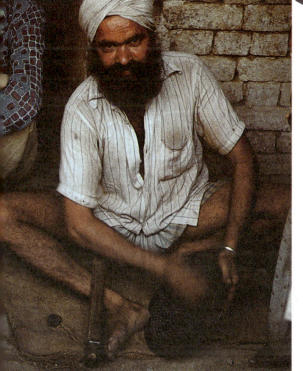

◀ The blacksmith makes tools for sale in the city.

The Granth was kept beneath a beautiful canopy in the village gurdwara.
▼

DEATH AND BIRTH

Early one morning the children woke at the usual time. It was half past six but something was wrong. There was not the usual bustle and noise of farmers on their way to the fields. Rema asked Balwant what had happened. Balwant explained that an old Sikh man had died during the night. He was a well liked and respected farmer. The whole village was upset by his death, even though he had been ill for some time.

The body of the dead man was washed and dressed. The five symbols of the Sikhs were all to be seen: the shorts, the steel bracelet, the sword by his side, the long hair and the comb. Amardip noticed that although people were very upset and some were crying there was no loud shouting and wailing. Instead people called out 'Wahiguru', which means 'wonderful Lord'.

The body was carried on a bier to be cremated. As the people followed the body they sang hymns. Relations of the dead man lit the wood at the funeral pyre. As the fire burned prayers were said for the dead. All the villagers walked back with the dead man's relatives. At their house the relatives thanked all those who had been to the funeral.

A Sikh funeral pyre.
▼

40

Balwant told Rema and Amardip that after two days the relatives would collect the ashes from the pyre and scatter them over the river. The Granth would be read in the dead man's home for ten days. At the end of that time all his friends would call at the house and share in karah prasad.

The funeral had just finished when a message was brought to Balwant. His brother's wife had given birth to a baby girl. The child was premature and very small, and she needed medical attention urgently. Balwant ran to his car and rushed to his brother's house to take the baby and her parents to the hospital in Amritsar. Balwant drove as fast as he could and they soon reached the hospital.

Within minutes the baby was in an incubator in the hospital and her mother resting in bed. Many Indian hospitals have very modern equipment. The doctor told the parents not to worry. The baby would live, thanks to Balwant's fast driving. Other babies in India might not be so lucky. They might be born in villages where no one owns a car and which are many kilometres from a hospital, although India is trying hard to provide health care for all the people. Amardip and Rema decided they would like to help in some way when they arrived home in Britain. Rema said she would have a toy sale at home and send the money to one of the organisations which helps children around the world.

The baby was rushed ▶
to hospital and
placed in an
incubator.

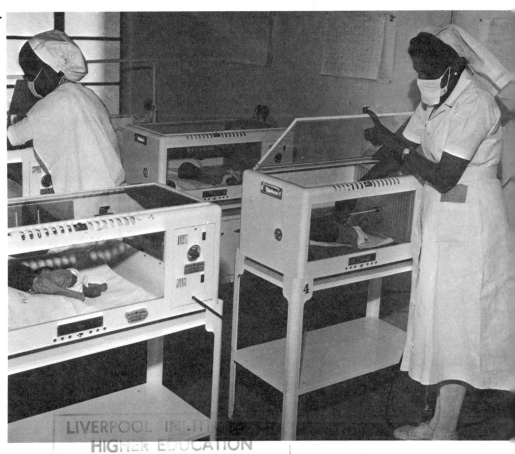

PREPARATIONS FOR GURU NANAK'S BIRTHDAY

The villagers were all delighted that the baby was safe. It meant they could prepare for one of the great days of the year without any worries. Sikhs all over the world celebrate the birthday of the first guru, Nanak.

Balwant drove the children into Amritsar to see the preparations. They visited a gurdwara where dozens of people were preparing food. Men were peeling vegetables, women were making hundreds of chapattis from a mountain of flour. Balwant told Amardip and Rema that the people preparing food would be there all day. There had to be an enormous amount of food because tomorrow there would be thousands of Sikhs arriving at the gurdwara.

Thousands of chapattis would be needed once the visitors began to arrive.

Temporary gurdwaras were constructed to hold the large numbers of worshippers.

The Granth was being read in every gurdwara.

Some of the music was provided by young Sikhs.

The three of them toured the city. They saw temporary gurdwaras which had been put up on open land. As night approached the streets filled with people. The celebrations were beginning and the gurdwaras were already full. People sang hymns, prayed and made their offerings of money, food and, of course, flowers. The holy book was being read in gurdwaras throughout the Punjab. In some gurdwaras Amardip noticed that the music was provided by young Sikhs. Balwant told him that a group of older musicians had played earlier in the evening, but that the young people liked to hear their own groups.

As they walked back to Balwant's car they passed house after house, all brightly lit. Many had fairy lights in the window; some had candles on the garden wall. Everyone was friendly, smiling and happy. Rema thought it not only looked beautiful but somehow it felt beautiful. It was very late by the time Balwant took them home. They were tired but excited: tomorrow was Guru Nanak's birthday and there would be lots more to do and see.

In the evening every house was lit with hundreds of candles.

GURU NANAK'S BIRTHDAY

It was a normal working day for many people in the Punjab. The Hindu villagers were looking forward to their own festivals, but today they were working as usual. Fishermen were out on the lake and women were planting rice in the fields. The Sikhs however were not working. They would all be joining in the celebrations.

While the Sikhs celebrate the birthday of Guru Nanak, other people of India are still at work. These women are planting rice.

Fishermen sail out into the middle of the lake to catch fish in their huge nets.

Rema wanted to know more about Guru Nanak. She knew he had started the religion but she wanted to know more about him.

Guru Nanak

Nanak was born in 1469 AD in a village in the Punjab. Most of the people in the Punjab were Muslims or Hindus. Nanak grew up with people from both religions. He read their books and learned about what they believed. Sikh parents tell their children of the amazing events that occurred when Nanak was small; how he was born with a smile on his face and surrounded by a bright light; how he could argue with his elders when he was only seven.

Nanak was not happy with either the Muslim or the Hindu religion. He used to say 'There is no Hindu and no Muslim. We are all brothers.' Nanak began to preach to people in the villages of the Punjab. He did not go alone. He went with an old Muslim called Hardana and a poor Hindu called Bala. Nanak travelled far and wide. He went as far south as Sri Lanka and as far west as Mecca in Arabia.

The Guru told people that the most important thing in life is what a person is like inside, not the way they appear on the outside. He taught that people should love everyone and be kind to all animals and birds. Everyone should speak the truth and work hard and honestly. Nanak told people that there is only one God, who judges people by what they do – not by their colour or whether they are rich or poor.

During his lifetime the followers of Nanak were still Muslims and Hindus. However, as time went by Sikhism developed into a separate religion.

'Today is very special for us,' Balwant told Rema. 'We do not worship Guru Nanak, we only worship God, but we do think about Guru Nanak and his teaching. It helps us to remember what we should do to be good Sikhs.'

Guru Nanak told his followers to remember God, to work hard and to help others.

BIRTHDAY CELEBRATIONS

Balwant and the children left the car on the edge of town. The streets were so busy it was impossible to drive any further. Amardip asked if they were going straight to where the food was being served. Balwant laughed and reminded Amardip that Sikhs eat after they have been to pray, not before.

The smile disappeared from Amardip's face as he stepped into the gurdwara courtyard. A fierce-looking man pointed a sword at him and called out in Punjabi. Balwant told Amardip to remove his sandals; he was on holy ground. The fierce man smiled and put his sword away. They all handed their shoes over to the man at the gate. Prayers go on all day and the Granth is read continuously. Most people join in for part of the day. As some worshippers leave, others arrive.

Amardip was challenged by a fierce-looking man with a sword.

The children left their shoes with an attendant before they entered the gurdwara.

All the Sikhs began their celebrations by joining in prayers.

Balwant led the children to the dining area. Hundreds of Sikhs were being fed at the same time. The food was served on plates made from leaves. Everyone ate as much as he liked. Rema realised why so many people had worked so hard preparing all the food. She could not believe that so many worshippers could all be fed as quickly as this. The children returned to the village that evening sleepy but contented. They had taken part in wonderful celebrations, very different from anything at home in Britain.

Their visit was now almost at an end. The children spent the following two days relaxing in the village. It had been a wonderful trip and both children had enjoyed it much more than they had expected. They would have so much to tell their friends – all about the things they had seen and experienced, and what they thought. Rema wondered how she could have had doubts about coming to India. From now on India would no longer be a faraway land; it was a real place with kind people who cared about them and who they would visit again one day.

Thousands of people were fed. The food was served on plates made from leaves.

TEACHER'S NOTES

The *At Home and Abroad* series is designed to start from what the child knows – Britain, and to move to the distant location. It is intended that the characters in the books are seen as brown/black British rather than the increasingly anachronistic 'immigrant'.

The text aims to introduce a number of key concepts. The table below lists the main ones but is not exhaustive.

Page
4/5   Change; cause and effect
6/7   Adaptation
8/9   Distance; location; adaptation
10/11   Values/beliefs
12/13   Adaptation
14/14   Similarity/difference
16/17   Change
18/19   Power; sex roles
20/21   Change; similarity/difference
22/23   Adaptation; location
24/25   Similarity/difference
26/27   Tradition; values/beliefs
28/29   Similarity/difference; scale; distance
30/31   Values/beliefs
36/37   Adaptation; change; cause and effect
38/39   Power; sex-roles; interdependence
40/41   Similarity/difference
42/43   Sex roles; tradition
44/45   Interdependence; values/beliefs
46/47   Continuity/change; tradition

The books are also intended to provide a vehicle for teachers to encourage pupils in the exploration of values and attitudes. It is hoped that these will include open-mindedness, evaluation, empathy, curiosity, exploration of attitudes and openness to change, an interest in human affairs, willingness to look for causes and tolerance for the belief systems of others.

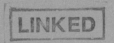